The Library of
NATIVE AMERICANS

# The Potawatomi

## of Wisconsin

### Damon Mayrl

The Rosen Publishing Group's
PowerKids Press™
New York

*To Mom and Dad*

The editors wish to thank Billy Daniels, Spiritual Leader of the Potawatomi tribe, for his expertise.

Published in 2003 by The Rosen Publishing Group, Inc.
29 East 21st Street, New York, NY 10010

Copyright © 2003 by The Rosen Publishing Group, Inc.

Photo and Illustration Credits: Cover and p. 28 Beloit College, Logan Museum of Anthropology, Beloit, WI (cover, 31077, p. 28, 30941); p. 4 Erica Clendening; pp. 7, 20, 22, 31 courtesy National Museum of the American Indian, Smithsonian Institution (p. 7, N26799, photo by Col. Frank C. Churchill; p. 20, D242165, photo by Katherine Fogden; p. 22, P22022; p. 31, S212723, photo by Janine Jones); pp. 8, 15, 16, 39, 43 courtesy Western History/Genealogy Department, Denver Public Library; p. 11 © Layne Kennedy/CORBIS; pp. 12, 32, 40 © Richard Hamilton Smith/CORBIS; pp. 27, 46 © Bettmann/CORBIS; pp. 34, 55 courtesy Photo Archives, Denver Museum of Nature and Science; p. 37 courtesy The Detroit Institute of the Arts, USA/Founders Society Purchase/Bridgeman Art Library; p. 44 Map and Geography Library and the Digital Imaging and Media Technology Initiative, University of Illinois Library at Urbana-Champaign; pp. 48, 51 © CORBIS; p. 52 © Joseph Sohm, ChromoSohm Inc./CORBIS.

Book Design: Erica Clendening

Mayrl, Damon.
     The Potawatomi of Wisconsin / by Damon Mayrl.
               p. cm. — (The library of Native Americans)
     Summary: Discusses the origins, social structure, spiritual beliefs, and daily life of the Potawatomi, as well as examining their contributions to American culture.
     Includes bibliographical references and index.
     ISBN 0-8239-6428-0
     1. Potawatomi Indians—Wisconsin—Juvenile literature. [1. Potawatomi Indians. 2. Indians of North America—Great Lakes Region.] I. Title. II. Series.
     E99.P8 M44 2002
     977.5004'923—dc21

                                                                  2002004091

*Manufactured in the United States of America*

*There are a variety of terminologies that have been employed when writing about Native Americans. There are sometimes differences between the original language used by a Native American group for certain names or vocabulary and the anglicized or modernized versions of such names or terms. Although this book contains terms that we feel will be most recognizable to our readership, there may also exist synonymous or native words that are preferred by certain speakers.*

# Contents

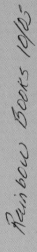

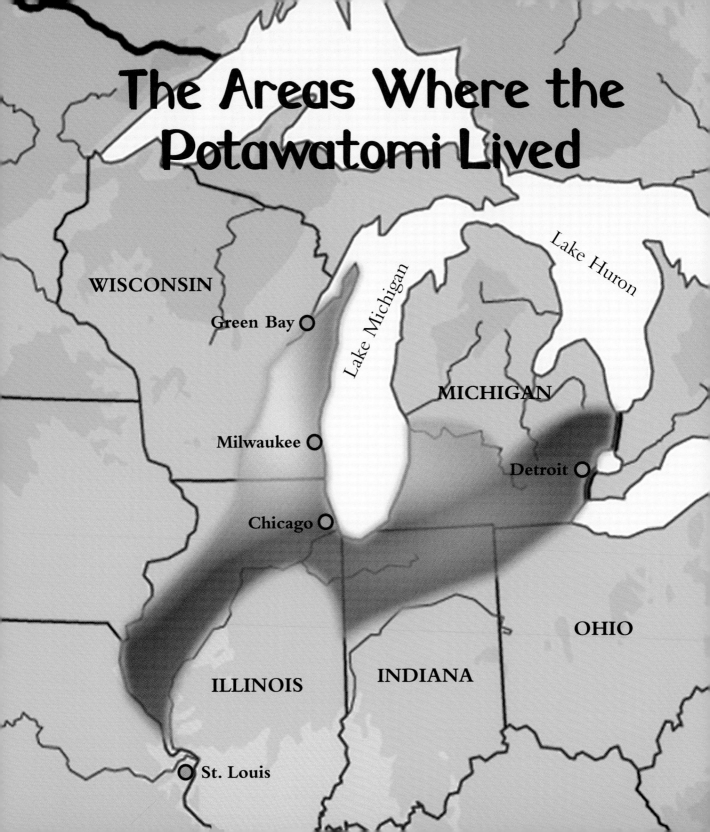

# The Areas Where the Potawatomi Lived

WISCONSIN

Green Bay ○

Lake Michigan

Lake Huron

MICHIGAN

Milwaukee ○

Detroit ○

Chicago ○

OHIO

ILLINOIS

INDIANA

○ St. Louis

# One

## Introducing the Potawatomi

Tens of thousands of years ago, human beings crossed into North America from Siberia. Over the years, they spread out across the continent. As they came to new lands, groups of them would decide to stop migrating and settle down. In the eastern region of what are today the United States and Canada, a vast forest stretched from the Atlantic Ocean to the Great Lakes. This forest was filled with birds, fruits, useful plants, and lakes and rivers with fish. Many of the migrating tribes saw it as an ideal place to live.

One of the tribes that came to live in the forest was called the Potawatomi. Potawatomi legend holds that they were originally part of an ancient tribe called the Anishnabe, who lived in Canada. One day, the Great Spirit came to the Anishnabe and told them to split into three groups. The Great Spirit gave each tribe a separate task. The Ojibwa, or "keepers of the faith," were responsible for maintaining the ancient tribe's religious beliefs. The Odawa, or "traders," were responsible for locating food and supplies. Finally, the group that came to be known as the Potawatomi was responsible for keeping the sacred fire burning. They acquired the name Potawatomi, which means "fire keepers." The Potawatomi refer to themselves as Neshnabe, or simply "the people."

This map shows the lands that the Potawatomi held at their peak, around 1812.

The Potawatomi were part of a group of Native American tribes called the Algonquian. The Algonquian lived in the eastern forest regions and had very similar cultures and spoke similar languages. The tribes did not always get along, however, and each tribe had distinctive traditions that separated it from the other tribes. The Potawatomi were no exception.

The first known records of the Potawatomi indicate that they originally lived in what is now lower Michigan. As a result of war among the Native American tribes, however, they soon moved to the other side of Lake Michigan and settled in what is now Wisconsin. There, they became one of the more powerful tribes in the region. At the height of their power, they controlled land from the Mississippi River in the west, to Lake Huron in the east, and from Green Bay in the north, to St. Louis in the south. They were known among other tribes as a very welcoming people, but a people who were proud and fierce in battle.

The Potawatomi played an important role in the development of the Great Lakes region. Potawatomi workers made the most of their fertile environment. Their society was bound together by religious rituals, group ceremonies, and strong families. As the group came in contact with other tribes and European colonists, the Potawatomi have kept the flame of their traditions burning. In many ways, they are indeed still the "keepers of the fire."

Generations of Potawatomi have passed on their knowledge and traditions. This is a photo of an elderly Potawatomi woman named Min-we-we-gishi-gok-we.

# Two
# Potawatomi Technology

The Potawatomi lived in villages during the warm growing season but traveled and hunted in the woods during the winter. Potawatomi villages were usually built on the edge of the forest, near prairies and lakes. Since the Potawatomi relied on rivers for much of their transportation, many villages were also built near rivers.

## Shelter

The most common form of shelter among the Potawatomi was the wigwam. These oval structures were about fifteen feet wide. The Potawatomi made wigwams by driving saplings, or small trees, into the ground and then tying them together at the top with strips of hide. They placed other saplings horizontally around the frame to reinforce the structure. They then placed mats made of woven grass around the outside of the frame. A hearth was built inside, and an opening was left at the top of the roof to let the smoke escape. On either side of the hearth, the Potawatomi slept on skins or low platforms.

The wigwam was a very effective shelter. The mats were very good at keeping out rain, snow, and wind. When the Potawatomi

This is a studio portrait of John Shab-e-nay, who belonged to the Prairie Band of the Potawatomi. He holds a beaded fringed bag and wears moccasins, leggings, a blanket, a cloth bandolier, metal armbands, beaded necklaces, and a top hat. This picture was taken between 1870 and 1880 in Holton, Kansas, when John was about twenty years old.

left their summer villages to go hunting during the winter, they would take the mats off of the frames, carry them, and use them to build new wigwams at their next campsite. They left the frames of their wigwams standing when they left each campsite, however, so they could use them when they returned to the same site again. Wigwams were easy to build. A wigwam could be built in around two hours, which was very convenient when the tribe was on its winter hunt.

During the summer, the Potawatomi also built larger houses covered in bark. These houses had high, arched roofs and were built around a frame of sturdy poles. These summer houses were cooler than the wigwams and could contain more people. The Potawatomi preferred to be outdoors during the summer and used these houses only as places to sleep or to avoid rain.

# Food

The forest in Wisconsin was a fertile land filled with food. During the summer, each Potawatomi woman had a small garden, where she grew beans, corn, squash, melons, peas, and tobacco. The men hunted in the area around the village. They would hunt buffalo, deer, elk, moose, bear, beavers, foxes, muskrats, and many different wild birds, such as partridges and wood hens. The men were also responsible for gathering wild rice from nearby marshes in their canoes. The women and children gathered

Elk were hunted by the Potawatomi.

12    Maple trees provided the Potawatomi with sap, which they used to make sugar, vinegar, and candy.

berries, nuts, and wild fruit during the summer to add to the food provided from the hunting and gardening.

Each autumn, the tribe broke up into families, left their villages, and went hunting in the forest. There, they were able to follow the tracks of game in the snow. At other times, the Potawatomi would catch animals with nets or special traps. One type of trap was a pit-fall, a concealed hole in the ground. Another type of trap was a deadfall, in which a heavy object was positioned to fall on and kill an animal. The Potawatomi used these various hunting techniques throughout the cold winter season.

In early spring, the Potawatomi gathered in groves of maple trees to collect sap. Maple sap was very important to the Potawatomi. Potawatomi children drank the sap straight from the tree or made candy by throwing sap into the snow. The sap was most useful, however, when it was boiled into syrup or dried into sugar, which was easier to store and carry. The Potawatomi often seasoned their food with this sugar or with vinegar made from maple sap that had been allowed to turn sour.

The large quantity of fish in Wisconsin's lakes and rivers provided another source of food throughout the year. Usually, the Potawatomi caught fish in nets or traps. Sometimes, however, a group of Potawatomi would go out in canoes at night and hunt fish by torch-light. The torches cast light into the clear waters of lakes and rivers, surprising the fish for a brief time. By temporarily stunning the fish, the Potawatomi were able to catch them with their spears.

During the winter, the Potawatomi mostly relied on small game and fish for their food. They also stored food for times when hunting did not supply them with enough food throughout the winter. During the summer, the Potawatomi buried extra sugar, berries, corn, beans, and peas in the ground in containers made of bark. Meat and fish caught during the summer were also dried or smoked and saved for use during the winter. The Potawatomi would mark the spot where they buried their food so they could find it and dig it up over the course of the winter, even when the ground was covered in snow.

The Potawatomi traditionally ate two meals a day. Normally, meals were simple and small. Meat and vegetables were roasted over a fire or boiled in birch bark containers. However, when there was an abundance of food, when visitors came to the village, or when a special ceremony was held, the village would come together for a huge feast. These feasts would be up to four courses.

# Clothing

Traditionally, the Potawatomi made their clothing from the hides of animals, such as buffalo and deer, that they caught on their hunts. The hides would be put through a tanning process, in which the skins would be treated to make them last longer. From these tanned hides, the Potawatomi made a wide array of clothes.

This is a studio portrait of John Maskwas, a Potawatomi man. He wears a kerchief with an oval medallion, several strands of white bead necklaces, a print shirt with ribbon trim, a metal arm band, a plaid, fringed blanket around his waist, leggings with diamond pattern beaded garters, and moccasins. He holds a fan of peacock feathers on his arm.

15

16    This studio portrait of a Potawatomi man was taken sometime between 1872 and
1879. He poses with his war club and fringed rifle sheath and wears moccasins,
leggings, a breechcloth, a quillwork shirt, and scarves in his braids.

Men's clothing consisted of a shirt and a breechcloth, or apron, worn with moccasins and leggings. Women wore buckskin dresses with a belt around their waists, moccasins, and leggings. To keep warm during the winter, both men and women wore heavy robes lined with fur. The Potawatomi women decorated their clothing with beautiful designs made from beads or embroidered with porcupine quills. After the Potawatomi came in contact with Europeans, they began to trade for brightly colored cloth. They made their clothes with the new materials instead of animal skins. They decorated the cloth with beads and ribbons.

Babies spent most of their first nine months on a cradle-board, a cedar board with a headbrace and a footrest. They were bound to the board in warm buckskin lined with sphagnum moss, which acted as a diaper. Small holes were cut in the soles of their moccasins so that if an evil spirit came to ask the infant to go on a journey with him, the baby could tell the spirit, "I can't go with you. I have holes in my moccasins."

The Potawatomi took great pride in their personal appearances and decorated their bodies as well as their clothes. Both men and women decorated their bodies with paint for ceremonial occasions, and men wore red and black paint when they went off to war. Men also decorated their bodies with tattoos.

# Tools

The Potawatomi fashioned many useful tools from the materials they found in their environment. Most of their tools were made from stone, bone, wood, and bark. Stones were useful for creating tools for chopping or shaping, such as axes, wedges, chisels, awls, and knives.

The Potawatomi made bows and arrows to use for hunting game. Most bows were about 4 feet (1.22 m) long and made of hard wood, such as white ash. The bow strings were made from deer hide. They made arrows from softer pine or cedar and decorated them with feathers. Arrowheads were usually made of flint, although at times bone or antler was used instead. To help them prepare animal hides for the tanning process, the Potawatomi made scrapers from bones. They used these scrapers to remove flesh from the skins. They also made troughs and wedges out of wood to collect sap from maple trees.

To work with their crops, the Potawatomi fashioned hoes and digging tools from wood. Corn was pounded into flour in wooden mortars. During the summer, women made mats out of birch bark, grass, and reeds to cover their wigwams. They sewed them together using string made from the bark of basswood and moose-wood trees or from the roots of pine trees. Since the Potawatomi ate most of their food with their hands, they did not need to create many tools for eating. They made bowls for soups out of wood, and spoons were made from wood, mussel shells, or birch bark. The Potawatomi scooped marrow from bones with a tool that they fashioned from a willow stick. Other pointed sticks were used to spear meat from hot stews.

The Potawatomi made many containers out of birch bark. A craftsman would heat a piece of bark and then bend it into a useful shape. The bark would then be sewn to keep its new shape. The Potawatomi created watertight birch bark containers for cooking, boiling, and holding liquid. Other containers were used for storing sugar, rice, fruit, and berries.

# Transportation

The Potawatomi devised many creative means of transportation. Each was designed to be used during a particular season. In the summer, the Potawatomi traveled mostly in canoes and dugouts. Dugouts were made simply by hollowing out the inside of a log with fire, but canoes took a long time to make. Most canoes were made from birch bark. The birch bark was collected in the spring, when it was easier to shape. A craftsman would build a frame for the canoe by bending cedar wood. He would then sew on large pieces of bark. To seal the canoe, the Potawatomi used pitch from pine trees. Although the Potawatomi canoes were light, they were able to carry remarkable amounts of material. Their lightness made them easier for the Potawatomi to portage, or carry from one river to another.

20    This Potawatomi yarn bag has a woven design called "Underwater Panther."

This allowed them to travel long distances quickly. When the Europeans started their fur trade, they found canoes so useful that they began using them as well.

During the winter, the Potawatomi used snowshoes to make travel easier on their long hunts. These shoes, made from bent ash sticks, enabled them to walk more quickly through deep snow. To carry materials, the Potawatomi also created sleds and toboggans from hides and lightweight wood. They loaded the toboggans with fire-wood or other materials, and pulled them across the snow.

After they began to trade with the Europeans, the Potawatomi started using metal implements instead of stone. They replaced their birch bark containers with metal and glass ones, and their stone cutting implements with iron knives. They also began to use horses as a means of transportation. Horses could carry them over land very quickly, and the Potawatomi soon began to travel more and more by horse and less by canoe.

# *Three*

## Government and Daily Life

Each Potawatomi village was led by four chiefs and a healer. When disagreements occurred, the chiefs called a meeting of the *wgema*, or tribal council. The *wgema* was a group made up of the oldest and wisest members of the community. After discussing the problem, the *wgema* would make a decision. The *wgema* always made the final decision to settle any disagreement.

## Families and Clans

The basic unit of Potawatomi society was the family. The family was made up of two parents and all of their unmarried children. Often, older relatives such as grandparents would live with the family. From time to time, other closely related members of the extended family would also come live with them, such as a married child and his or her spouse.

Each family was considered part of a clan. A clan consisted of groups of families who were related to one another by Potawatomi tradition. Each clan had a ritual name connected to the tribe's mythology. The clan served as an extended family for the Potawatomi. A group of clans would be organized into a larger group, called a phratry. These phratries of closely-linked clans worked together for ceremonial purposes.

This is a portrait of a Potawatomi woman and children from Mayetta, Kansas.

The Potawatomi defined their families very broadly. Cousins on both sides of the family were considered "brothers" and "sisters," a father and his brothers were known as "father," and a mother and her sisters were known as "mother." Each person was expected to behave in a certain way to other members of their family. Potawatomi children were expected to be respectful of their parents, brothers, sisters, and parents-in-law. They were also expected to show respect for those who were older.

Potawatomi families grew either through marriages or through ceremonial adoptions. Marriages were usually arranged between families to create bonds between them. Although most marriages were between one man and one woman, it was possible for a Potawatomi man to have more than one wife. When a man took a second wife, she was often the sister of his first wife.

Ceremonial adoptions took place when a member of the tribe died. To replace the dead relative, a person who was not part of the clan was adopted into the family. Frequently, the adopted person was a friend of the relative who had died. Although he or she did not come to live in the household with the adopting family or join the clan, he or she took on the rights and responsibilities that the dead individual had to the family and clan. Through both marriage and ceremonial adoption, the Potawatomi clans were brought closer together, which reduced conflict.

Men and women had separate duties in a Potawatomi village. Women were responsible for tending the garden, cooking, setting up the house, making clothing, and taking care of the children. Men were responsible for hunting, fishing, trapping, trading, and fighting enemy tribes when necessary. Children were taught their responsibilities as they grew up. Boys fished and hunted small game, while girls helped their mothers with the household tasks.

# Games and Sports

The Potawatomi played a number of games for amusement. Some of these games were religious or ceremonial, and played to honor certain spirits, while others were just for fun. The most important game to the Potawatomi was lacrosse. Traditionally, lacrosse was a sacred game for the Potawatomi. Only men were allowed to play. A member of the tribe would sponsor a game of lacrosse in honor of his guardian spirit. He sent gifts of tobacco to ten men and threw a big celebration feast on the day of the match. The game was played on a field with a goal post on each end, one for each team. Every player had a long stick with a netted scoop at one end. The players used the scoops to pick a ball off the ground and the net to throw and catch the ball to one another. Each player tried to hit the opposite team's goal with the ball without using his hands. The game was played until five goals were scored. The sponsor had five prizes, which he gave to the players who scored the goals. The Europeans enjoyed playing lacrosse as well, and it is still played by the Potawatomi and other Americans today.

Although women were not allowed to play lacrosse, they had a similar game called double-ball. Double-ball was nearly the same as lacrosse, except that it was played with two balls joined together instead of just one ball. The Potawatomi women also played a game of dice to honor their guardian spirits. The women would shake together eight dice in a bowl. Each die was flat and circular, colored red on one side and blue on the other, except for one die that was shaped like a horse and another one that was shaped like a turtle. The women received points depending on the color pattern that turned up on each shake.

Older men sometimes played archery games. These games took several forms. The most popular of these games was played by four people divided into two teams. One player on each team constructed a mound and placed a colorful target on top. The other player then shot two arrows at the target. If neither player hit his target, the player who came closer won one point for his team. If one player hit the target with one arrow, his team won five points. If one player hit the target with both arrows, his team won ten points and the game. If both players hit the target with the same number of arrows, neither team won any points.

In another game played for entertainment, a group would come together with a pile of 201 straws about two inches long. The straws were then sorted into 19 bundles of 10 and one bundle of 11. These bundles were then mixed around. Each player would take a bundle, and whoever took the bundle of 11 was declared the winner and awarded a certain number of points. The Potawatomi particularly enjoyed this game and tournaments could last several days.

Another favorite game among the Potawatomi was known as the moccasin game. One player arranged six moccasins in front of him or her. Then, singing and moving quickly to distract the other players' attention, he or she would hide a small colored stick beneath one of the moccasins. The other players then placed bets on which moccasin was covering the stick.

This is an illustration of a Native American lacrosse player. Lacrosse was played by many groups in North America.

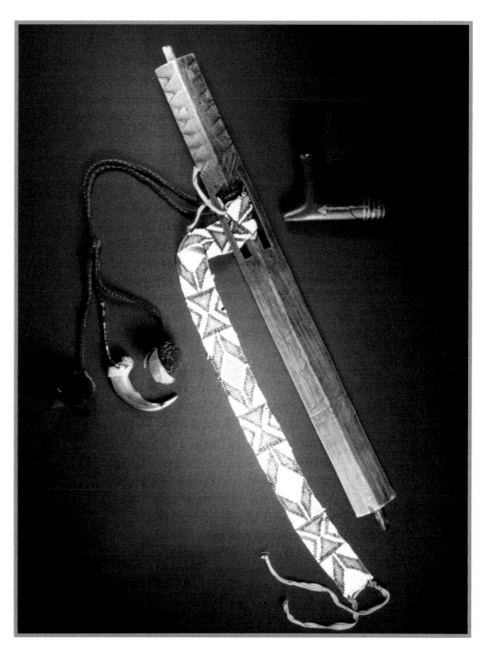

This photo shows a Potawatomi pipe and decorated accessories.

# Arts and Crafts

The Potawatomi were very skilled at making beautiful art to decorate the objects they created. The most traditional type of decoration was quillwork, which was practiced only by Native American tribes living in the forests. Quills from porcupines were sewn into animal skins or woven in intricate patterns. After the men had killed a porcupine, the women would remove the quills and sort them by length and thickness. The Potawatomi dyed them red, black, yellow, and blue, using the roots and bark of local plants. Through wrapping, sewing, and weaving, the Potawatomi were able to create beautiful and colorful designs from the porcupine quills.

Beadwork was another specialty of the Potawatomi. Traditionally, the Potawatomi made beads from small shells or from pieces of bone. However, after the Europeans arrived, the Potawatomi began to use glass beads. The Potawatomi took inspiration for their designs from nature. To create the patterns for their beadwork, women would rub the backs of leaves with charcoal. Then they would press the leaves on a piece of white birch bark to create a pattern. They would sew the beads into place according to this pattern. The Potawatomi used both weaving and embroidering to create their beadwork designs.

The Potawatomi were accomplished weavers. In addition to weaving with quills and beads, Potawatomi women wove mats, bags, and baskets out of bark fiber, wild grasses, and, later, yarn. These items were often woven in beautiful designs, and weaving is still a popular craft among the Potawatomi today.

After the arrival of the Europeans, the Potawatomi began to create artwork from materials they received through trade, such as silk ribbons and silver. One new technique the Potawatomi used to decorate their clothing was called silk appliqué. The Potawatomi would cut pieces of silk that they received in trade from Europeans and attach them to the edges of their garments. They also learned how to work with silver, and they began to create fine silver brooches, bracelets, earrings, and other jewelry.

This photo shows a corn husk doll made by the Potawatomi.

# Four

# Potawatomi Religion

The Potawatomi believed the world was filled with *manidos*, or spirits. *Manidos* lived in everything that made up the Potawatomi's environment. There were *manidos* that lived in fire, the sun, the moon, thunder, lightning, the four winds, and eagles. Other spirits lived in rocks, plants, and animals. While some *manidos* were good, others were evil. Each of them was powerful and commanded respect. The Potawatomi frequently made offerings of tobacco and food to good *manidos* to seek their help, to thank them for their generosity, and to keep the evil spirits away.

The bear *manido* commanded a great deal of respect. The Potawatomi had a special ceremony they performed whenever they killed a bear during their hunting. The bear's head and hide would be laid out, along with fine clothing. The tribe would have a special feast in which tobacco and fresh food would be offered to the spirit of the bear. A speaker would address the other wild bears and promise that all the bears that they killed in the future would receive equally fine treatment. After the bear was eaten, its bones were carefully gathered and piled up, not left scattered about as with other animals. In this way, the Potawatomi made peace with the spirit world while continuing to live from the land.

The Potawatomi believed that spirits inhabited the natural world.

In addition to *manidos* that lived in nature, each individual was thought to have a personal *manido*, or guardian spirit. When boys and girls reached adulthood, they fasted for four days in the hope of receiving a vision from their guardian spirit. This vision quest was very important to the Potawatomi. They believed that a vision could show what events would take place

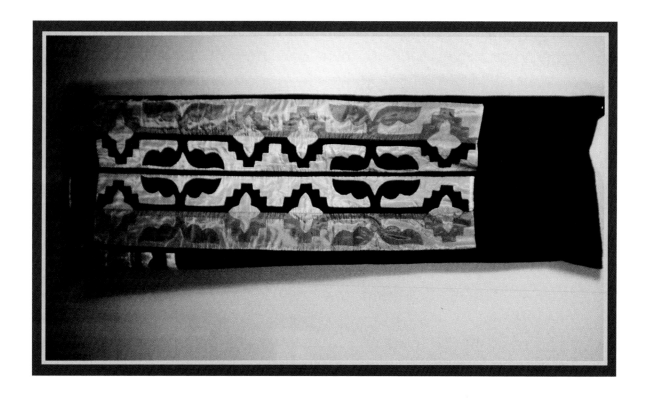

34  This photo shows Potawatomi ribbonwork sewn on muslin and attached to a blanket robe.

in a person's life and that any objects that appeared in the dream could provide special help or protection to the dreamer. Over the course of his or her life, each Potawatomi would make offerings to his or her guardian spirit on a regular basis, in the hope that the spirit would provide him or her with good favor, a successful hunt, or other good things.

One of the most powerful spirits was called Wiske. Wiske was a powerful spiritual force who both played tricks on the Potawatomi and brought them good things. They believed that Wiske had given the Potawatomi tobacco and corn, and taught them about plants in the forest that could be used for medicine. Wiske was also believed to have established the clan system. Sometimes the Potawatomi called Wiske the "Master of Life" because of his importance in shaping their lives. The Potawatomi told many stories about Wiske's adventures. Each season had its own set of stories told only during that time.

Like many other Native American tribes, the Potawatomi believed in an afterlife. They thought that a person had two souls, one that went to heaven and one that stayed on earth. When a person died, one soul took a four-day journey to heaven, which lay to the west. During its journey, Chibiabos, the younger brother of Wiske, would help the soul until it reached heaven.

# Religious Ceremonies

The Potawatomi had a number of religious ceremonies. These ceremonies were held to help cure the sick, to call on the powers of the *manidos*, or to bring the community together. The most important of these was the Medicine Dance, which was held twice a year by the Midewiwin, or Grand Medicine Society. The Midewiwin was a group of people who used a special ritual to help cure the sick. When a person became sick, sometimes he would be told by a spirit to join the society. In that case, he went through a special initiation in which he joined the society and learned the curing ritual. The Midewiwin performed the Medicine Dance to celebrate when new members joined the group.

Another important traditional ceremony was called the Brave Dance. The Brave Dance was held before men went off to war. The warriors called the community together for a Brave Dance to pray to their guardian spirits for protection and good luck. They dedicated food and tobacco to the *manidos* and held a great feast, followed by singing and dancing.

In more recent times, a religious ceremony was held that was adopted from other Native American tribes from the Great Plains to the West. It was called the Dream Dance, and it was performed around a large drum. The drum, which was called "Our Grandfather," was thought to have powerful supernatural properties. The songs and rituals in the Dream Dance were meant to bring power and honor to the tribe. On the day of the dance, a speaker made a speech to the spirit of the drum, praising the spirit for its virtues, such as peace, responsibility, and good moral conduct. Then the tribe celebrated by singing, dancing, playing the drum, and exchanging gifts with one another. Often, people passed a *calumet*, or peace pipe, between one another to end fighting and promote friendship.

This Potawatomi prescription stick was carved out of wood.

# Life Ceremonies

The Potawatomi performed a number of ceremonies to observe special times in an individual's life and after an individual's death. Among the important rituals in a Potawatomi's life were the naming feast, the feast of the first game, and marriage.

The naming feast occurred when a child was very young. The parents asked an older man or woman to name their child. The namer then offered tobacco and food to his or her guardian spirit and chose the name, which he or she would have received in a dream. It was considered a great honor to name a child, and the namer and the child had a special relationship for the rest of their lives.

The feast of the first game was given only for boys. It occurred when they had their first successful hunting experience. A boy's parents would invite friends and relatives for a feast, where they would give offerings to the spirit of the dead animal. Every person ate a little of the animal, except for the boy who had killed it. The feast was held so that he would have success in hunting as he grew older.

Marriage was a simple affair. In the Potawatomi tradition, if a man wished to marry a woman, he simply brought a blanket to her home. If she agreed to wear the blanket, they were married. A feast would be held, and the two families would exchange presents. Then the two would live together. A couple who wished to divorce could do so just as easily. One member of the couple would simply move out of the house.

The Potawatomi also had a special funeral ritual. The dead man or woman was dressed in his or her finest clothes and surrounded with his or her favorite possessions. A priest would speak to the dead person's spirit, describing the journey that he or she was about to take. A fire was built at the head of the grave, and tobacco was offered to Chibiabos. Four days later, a feast was held to celebrate the soul's arrival in heaven. A small house was built over the grave to provide a place for the earthly soul to rest.

This studio portrait of a Potawatomi man shows him holding a feather fan and wearing moccasins, leggings, bead necklaces, a turban, and a feather in his hair.

# Five

## History

The Potawatomi originally lived in what is now Lower Michigan. In the early part of the seventeenth century, however, the Iroquois nation, a group of tribes from what is now New York State, began to move west into Potawatomi territory. They came in search of furs to trade with Europeans, who had begun to build settlements on the Atlantic coast. The Potawatomi and their neighbors fought the Iroquois. However, the Iroquois had a deadly new weapon: the gun. Without guns of their own, the Potawatomi were unable to win battles against the Iroquois. The Potawatomi were quickly driven out of their lands. They fled to the north and west. There, about 3,000 Potawatomi took refuge on a chain of islands between Lake Michigan and what is now Green Bay.

The Menomonee and Winnebago tribes occupied the land on the other side of Lake Michigan. An epidemic had recently struck their tribes, and many of their people had died. The Menomonee and Winnebago were too weakened to stop the Potawatomi from coming to live on their lands, so they made peace with them. The Potawatomi began to build a new life on the new land, which was rich in wild rice, fish, and game.

Rock Island in Lake Michigan, Wisconsin, was home to Potawatomi who were driven from their lands.

# Trade with Europeans

In 1641, traders from France visited the Potawatomi. They had traveled across the Atlantic Ocean and through the Great Lakes region in search of furs and a passageway to Asia. The French found the Potawatomi to be expert trappers and honest traders. They began to trade beads, cloth, metal objects, and other goods to the Potawatomi in exchange for furs. The French and the Potawatomi formed a strong alliance. Soon the Potawatomi controlled much of the fur trade between France and the tribes of the western Great Lakes.

With the help of the French, the Potawatomi were able to move into land belonging to other tribes. By 1696, the Potawatomi and several other tribes had forced the Iroquois out of the western Great Lakes. Without a strong enemy to stand in their way, the Potawatomi quickly expanded their territory south along the Lake Michigan shoreline and then along rivers to the south and east. By 1770, they controlled land from present-day Detroit in the east, to what is now St. Louis in the west. As their lands grew, so did their population. By 1820, the Potawatomi numbered about 10,000, living in 100 villages.

Trading with the French caused dramatic changes in Potawatomi society. Before the French came, the Potawatomi spent most of their time finding food and other supplies that they needed. After they began to trade with the French, however, the

In this photo, probably taken between 1870 and 1880, a Potawatomi man wears a fur pelt blanket, bead necklaces, a medal, a shell pendant, and a turban.

43

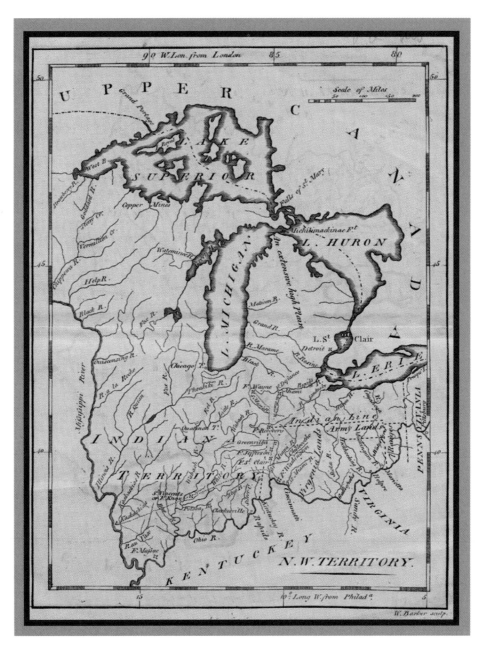

44    This 1801 map of the Northwest Territory outlines rivers, lakes, Indian territory, and military territory in present-day Wisconsin, Michigan, and Illinois.

tribe began to focus more on collecting furs to trade for European goods. The Potawatomi began to use European materials such as silver, iron, and cloth. Many Potawatomi women married French traders and the Potawatomi culture took on many French influences. Some Potawatomi became Christians, although most of them continued to believe in their traditional religion.

Unfortunately for the Potawatomi, however, the French were not the only Europeans who wanted to trade in the Great Lakes region. The English had also set up colonies in North America, and they went to war with the French for control of the land. Both sides made alliances with Native American tribes, and the Potawatomi sided with the French. The Potawatomi fought many battles against the English in the Seven Years' War, also known as the French and Indian War, but the French were forced out of North America in 1763. After the French defeat, some Potawatomi, including those in Wisconsin, continued to attack English trading forts. Others allied themselves with the English and began to trade with them.

Although they had lost their French trading partners, the Potawatomi had gained new English ones. However, this would not last. The English colonies on the Atlantic coast declared independence in 1776, and by 1783, the English had been driven out of the area around Lake Michigan.

46  This is a portrait of Tecumseh (1768?-1813), the Shawnee leader who helped the
Potawatomi resist settlers.

# The Potawatomi Lose Land to the United States

The new United States of America claimed Potawatomi lands as part of their new Northwest Territory. The Americans were hungry for new land to farm, and their growing population was eager to move onto the Potawatomi's land. The Potawatomi and other tribes in the Northwest Territory joined together to try to keep the American settlers off their lands. They were successful until 1794, when they suffered a major defeat at the Battle of Fallen Timbers, near what is now Toledo, Ohio. The following year, the Native American tribes were forced to give up some of their land to the Americans.

By 1807, many tribes had lost large amounts of land to the Americans. As a result, many American settlers moved into the Northwest Territory. The number of new American settlers alarmed the Potawatomi. Around this time, Tecumseh and Tenskwatawa, two leaders from the Shawnee tribe in Ohio, called on the tribes of the Northwest Territory to join together to resist the Americans. Many young Potawatomi listened to them and wanted to fight against the Americans. In 1811, they began a new war against the settlers. The following year, their English allies also went to war with the Americans in the War of 1812. At first, the war went very well, and the Native Americans defeated settlers across the Northwest Territory. But Tecumseh was killed in battle in 1813, and England made peace with the United States in 1814. The last major attempt by the Potawatomi to defeat the Americans had failed.

Between 1795 and 1833, the Potawatomi lost all of their land in the United States to the U.S. government. In 1830, the government declared a new policy toward Native Americans. This law said that

This 1877 photo shows Pisehedwin, a Potawatomi, and others in front of his Kansas farm home.

all Native American tribes east of the Mississippi River, including the Potawatomi, would have to move to the western side of the river. As part of this exchange, the government set aside land in Iowa and Missouri for the Potawatomi and promised to take care of the tribe.

Many Potawatomi packed up their belongings and moved west. Those who moved were eventually resettled in small reservations in Kansas and Oklahoma. However, not all of the Potawatomi left. Some refused, and instead fled north into remote parts of Wisconsin and Michigan, where they could hide. Some went even farther and fled into Canada, where they went to live in Odawa and Ojibwa villages. As a result, by the beginning of the twentieth century, the Potawatomi were split up and spread out across the United States and Canada.

## The Twentieth Century

By 1900, the Potawatomi who had stayed in Wisconsin were living in the northeastern part of the state. They were known as the "strolling Potawatomi," since they had no land of their own and were forced to move around from place to place. In 1913, the United States government officially recognized the Potawatomi of Wisconsin and gave them reservation land in Forest County. Unlike the Potawatomi who had moved to Kansas and Oklahoma, the Potawatomi of Wisconsin were able to maintain more of their traditions. This is because they were able to continue to live in forests rather than on the prairie, and because they had fewer conflicts with American settlers in their remote corner of Wisconsin.

Although the United States government gave the Potawatomi some support on the reservation, life was still very difficult. The Potawatomi's traditional ways of living had been largely destroyed. For example, although the government built new houses for the Potawatomi on the reservation, only one couple could live in each house. As a result, many families were broken up, and grandparents no longer lived with their grandchildren. It became much more difficult to pass on Potawatomi customs when the generations were separated, and many children grew up not hearing the tribal stories and participating in traditional cultural activities.

Many Potawatomi also found it difficult to earn a living during the twentieth century. The land that they received in Forest County had very little forest left on it, since lumber companies had cut down most of the old trees. The number of deer and fish had decreased, and the Potawatomi found it harder to survive off of the land. Many Potawatomi moved to cities, where they took jobs in factories. Later, they worked as skilled tradesmen. Members of the tribe who chose to stay on the reservation made their living through low-paying jobs, such as harvesting crops on nearby farms, working at lumber mills, and making arts and crafts for tourists. They remained very poor throughout much of the twentieth century.

These Native American women—from left to right, Minnie Spotted Wolf (Blackfoot), Celia Mix (Potawatomi), and Viola Eastman (Chippewa)—were reservists in the U.S. Marine Corps during World War II.

# Six

# The Potawatomi Today

Today, the Potawatomi have overcome many of the obstacles of their past and have become more prosperous. In 1988, the United States Congress passed the Indian Gaming Regulatory Act, which allowed the Potawatomi to permit gambling on their lands. The Potawatomi of Wisconsin built two casinos, one on their own reservation and another in Milwaukee. The casinos generate a lot of money and many jobs. The money the tribe makes through the casinos has enabled it to start many programs to help its people. Money from the casinos has been used to provide health care, education, day care, children's services, elderly services, housing improvements, and environmental protection on the tribal reservation. As jobs have come to the reservation, some of the Potawatomi who left for the cities in the past have begun to return. The reservation in Forest County is now home to over 500 Potawatomi.

The Potawatomi have also taken advantage of their new wealth to ensure that their traditions are preserved. The tribe has set up cultural centers and museums to provide information for new generations about the tribe's traditional customs. They have created a number of programs in which the tribe's elders are able to pass on the many Potawatomi stories and legends to younger members of

The modern-day Potawatomi have lands in Wisconsin, as well as Kansas, Oklahoma, Michigan, and Ontario, Canada. Pictured here is the Wisconsin River.

the tribe. Other programs have also been started to preserve the Potawatomi language, culture, and religion in the future.

Today, about 1,000 Potawatomi live in Wisconsin, while thousands more live in Kansas, Oklahoma, Michigan, and Ontario. Although they are spread out, members of the entire nation come together once a year for a gathering. At the gathering, the Potawatomi from the various reservations talk about language and traditional customs, and celebrate their common spiritual tradition. These gatherings are a time of joy and celebration and an opportunity to celebrate the nation's rich past, while building its future.

These Potawatomi moccasins were made of wide, soft leather. They are decorated with beads in the design of blue, green, and orange flowers. The cuff of the moccasins has a thin beaded edge.

55

# Timeline

| | |
|---|---|
| **Early 1600s** | Potawatomi are driven from Lower Michigan by the Iroquois and take refuge in northeastern Wisconsin. |
| **1641** | French traders first make contact with the Potawatomi. |
| **1763** | France loses the Seven Years' War against England and is forced out of North America. |
| **1776** | United States declares its independence from England. |
| **1783** | England gives up land in the Northwest Territory, including Potawatomi land, to the new United States. |
| **1794** | Potawatomi and their allies lose the Battle of Fallen Timbers and begin to lose their land to the American settlers. |
| **1795–1833** | Potawatomi lose more land to the United States and move to reservations in Kansas and Oklahoma. |
| **1813** | Tecumseh, leader of the Native American alliance, dies fighting the United States in the War of 1812. |

1913    "Strolling Potawatomi" are recognized by U.S. government and given reservation land in Forest County, Wisconsin.

1988    U.S. Congress passes Indian Gaming Regulatory Act.

1991    Potawatomi open a casino in Milwaukee, Wisconsin.

# Glossary

**afterlife** (AF-tur-lyfe)   A life or existence believed to follow death.

**Algonquian** (al-GAWN-kwee-ehn)   A name for all the Native American tribes of the Great Lakes region who spoke similar languages and had similar cultures.

**alliance** (uh-LY-uhns)   An agreement between two people or nations to work together.

**Anishnabe** (ah-nish-NAH-bay)   The name of the ancient tribe that became the Potawatomi, Ojibwa, and Odawa tribes.

**awls** (AWLS)   Pointed tools that are used to make holes.

**breechcloth** (BREECH-kloth)   A type of clothing that covers a man's midsection. It is made from a piece of cloth strung under and over a belt worn around the waist.

*calumet* (KAL-yuh-meht)   A pipe that was passed among members of the tribe to promote friendship.

**Chibiabos** (CHEE-bee-ah-bohs)   The spirit that escorted Potawatomi souls to heaven.

**clan** (KLAN)   A group of people related by blood or marriage.

**culture** (KUHL-chur)   The sum of all products of human life.

**deadfalls** (DEHD-fawls)   Hunting traps that kill an animal by crushing it under a heavy weight.

**lacrosse** (luh-KRAWS)   A traditional Native American game played with a ball and netted sticks.

*manido* (man-EE-doo)   A spirit that lives in nature.

**Midewiwin** (mih-DAY-ween)   A healing society that sponsored the Medicine Dance.

**Neshnabe** (nihsh-na-BAY)   Literally "the people"; the term that the Potawatomi use to call themselves.

**phratry** (FRAY-tree)   A collection of clans that are related to one another.

**pitfalls** (PIHT-falls)   Animal traps consisting of a hole in the ground hidden by leaves and branches.

**portage** (POHR-tihdj)   The technique of carrying a canoe from one river to another.

**quillwork** (KWIHLL-wurk)   A type of decoration made by weaving, sewing, wrapping, or plaiting porcupine needles.

**reservation** (reh-zur-VAY-shuhn)   Land set aside by the United States government for Native American tribes.

**seminomadic** (seh-mee-noh-MA-dihk)   A people who live in one place part of the time, but move from place to place at other times.

**silk appliqué** (SIHLK ap-pluh-KAY)   A type of decoration made by adding strips of silk or ribbon to a piece of clothing.

**tanning** (TA-ning)   The process of treating an animal skin in order to make it into a piece of clothing.

**tattoo** (ta-TOO)   Marks or designs made on the skin.

*wgema* (oh-GAH-mah)   The tribal council that made important decisions in Potawatomi villages.

**wigwam** (WIHG-wahm)   An oval-shaped type of house the Potawatomi used for shelter.

**Wiske** (wee-SKEH)   The cultural hero of the Potawatomi, who gave them corn and tobacco, but who also played jokes on them.

# Resources

## BOOKS

Clifton, James A. *The Potawatomi*. Broomall, PA: Chelsea House Publishers, 1987.

Edmunds, R. David. *The Potawatomis: Keepers of the Fire*. Norman, OK: University of Oklahoma Press, 1978.

Powell, Suzanne. *The Potawatomi*. New York: Franklin Watts, 1997.

Ritzenthaler, Robert E., and Pat Ritzenthaler. *The Woodland Indians of the Western Great Lakes*. Milwaukee, WI: Milwaukee Public Museum, 1983.

Whelan, Gloria. *Night of the Full Moon*. New York: Stepping Stone Books, 1996.

## MUSEUM

**Potawatomi Museum and Cultural Center**
5460 Everybody's Road
Crandon, WI 54520
(715) 478-7474

61

# WEB SITES

Due to the changing nature of Internet links, PowerKids Press has developed an online list of Web sites related to the subject of this book. This site is updated regularly. Please use this link to access the list:

www.powerkidslinks.com/lna/potawatomi

# Index